T.D. Jakes Speaks to Women!

Deliverance for the past,
healing for the present.

BISHOP T.D. JAKES

To: Barbara
From: Robin
"97"

T.D. Jakes Speaks to Women!
Deliverance for the past,
healing for the present.
ISBN 1-88008-987-4
Copyright © 1996 by T.D. Jakes
Dallas, Texas 75211

Published by ALBURY PUBLISHING
P.O. Box 470476
Tulsa, Oklahoma 74147-0406

Introduction

Few church leaders are ministering God's message of deliverance and restoration to the needs of women today like T.D. Jakes. Bishop Jakes' biblical message on the true nature of womanhood and his soothing words to the used and abused are a clarion call to the church.

We have tried to capture some of T.D. Jakes' most inspiring messages on womanhood in this convenient quote book. Whether it is read at home, or during a break at work, it is our hope that these bite size nuggets of wit and wisdom will encourage women everywhere to celebrate their womanhood. Celebrate your womanhood — with T.D. Jakes!

*M*y daughters are in their springtime, my wife is in the middle of summer, and my mother is walking through autumn to step into winter. Together they form a chord of womanhood—three different notes creating a harmonious blend.

*I*t is important to remember that for every person, there will be a problem. Even more importantly, for every problem, our God has a prescription!

*T*he more you medicate the symptoms,
the less chance you have of
allowing God to heal you.

*C*linging to people is far different from loving them.... It is taking and not giving.... God proved His love, not by His need of us, but by His giving to us.

It is wonderful to be self-sacrificing, but watch out for self-disdain! If you don't take some of the medicine you are healing others with, your patients will be healed while you are dying.

The glory of God is manifested only when there is a balance between grace and truth.

*I*t does not matter if you have been
oppressed socially, sexually,
or racially; our Lord is an
eliminator of distinctions.

*E*very woman has something she wishes she could forget.

*F*orgetting isn't a memory lapse; it is a memory release! Like carbon dioxide the body can no longer use, exhale the past and let it go out of your spirit.

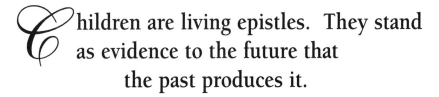

*C*hildren are living epistles. They stand as evidence to the future that the past produces it.

We can build all the churches we want. We can decorate them with fine tapestry and ornate artifacts. But if people cannot find a loving voice within our hallowed walls, they will pass through unaltered by our clichés and religious rhetoric.

*E*very time you see a woman who has unnatural fear in her eyes, low self-esteem, or an apologetic posture, she is saying, "Carest thou not that I perish?"

*Y*ou may right now be looking child abuse in the face. If you think it's ugly, you're right.... But if you think it can't be healed, you're dead wrong!

*Y*ou are standing in a stream with
water rushing around your ankles.
The waters that pass you by at that moment,
you will never see again. So it is with
the misery that has challenged your life.
Let it go, let it rush on by.

The only hospital for wounded souls is the Church.

*W*e must maintain a strong boundary line between our past and present. God is present.

*W*e will never know who a person
truly is, until we understand
where they have been.

*F*acing the past is the secret of being transformed from a vulnerable victim to a victorious, loving person. Be responsible enough to face your weaknesses and pains.

*T*here is a call out in the Spirit for hurting women.... No matter how many men have told you, "I don't want you," God says, "I want you." He says, "I've seen you bent over. I've seen you at your worst in the aftereffects of what's happened to you. And still, I want you."

*A*llow God's power and anointing to touch your hurting places. God knows the woman you would have been, should have been, and could have been. So let Him heal and restore you as you call out to Him.

*F*orget how many times you've been married. Put aside those who mistreated you. You can't change where you've been, but you can change where you are going.

*W*omen are open beings by nature and design. Men are closed. So be careful who you open yourself up to. Those who seek your help may drain your power.

*T*here is a special conflict between the woman and Satan. He is attracted to you because he knows that you were designed as a receptacle to help meet someone's vision. If he can get you to help meet his vision, you will have great problems.

*U*ntil the desire to go forward becomes
greater than the memories of past
pain, you will never hold the power
to create again.

*T*oo often we starve the embryo of faith that is growing within us. Put God's truth in your spirit and let it feed. Allow it to nurture and grow.

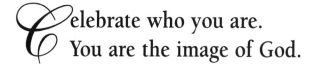
Celebrate who you are.
You are the image of God.

God wants us to understand that just because we can't see it, doesn't mean that He won't do it.

*G*od will reward those who persevere in seeking Him. He may not come when you want Him to. But He will be right on time.

*W*hy should you allow your vision to be incapacitated for lack of a man? Cling to the truth that God is doing a good work in *you*. Each of us needs our own vision and walk with God.

Woman, you do make a difference.
The world would be a different
place if it were not for you.

*O*ften, unmarried women complain of their need for a husband. But rarely does a single woman boast about the kind of relationship she is free to build with the Lord. So before you ask God again for a man, take care of Him.

The Scripture calls unmarried women virgins because God is of the opinion that if you do not belong to a man, you belong strictly to Him. Single women ought to be the most consecrated women in the church.

When you confront your husband, don't make him feel interrogated. Remember, you could win the argument and still lose the man.

*M*en created in the likeness of God respond well to praise. A woman who knows how to talk to a man is difficult to withstand.

If you are looking for someone to be
your everything, don't look around.
Look up!

A truly good relationship is a spicy meal
served on a shaky table, filled
with dreams and pains and tender moments.
Moments that in those split-second flash-
backs, make you smile secret smiles in
the middle of the day.

*M*any see Jesus as a way to heaven and the solution to spiritual problems. But they fail to see that He is the solution to *all* of life's problems.

*F*aith is more than a fact — faith is an action.

*W*oman, God wants you to believe
Him. Make a quality decision
and stand on it.

*R*egardless of your social position or your past, God raises people up equally.

If you have blown it, know that God
is in the business of restoring
broken lives.

*I*f you believe your past can keep
you from moving forward with
God, you underestimate the power of faith.

If you want the enemy to release you, remind him Whose daughter you are.

*G*od is no respecter of persons.
Faith is based on equal opportunity.

*T*he power to get wealth is in your tongue. You shall have whatever you say.

And all things, whatsoever ye shall ask in prayer, believing, ye shall receive. Matthew 21:22

*I*t's not what people think and say
about you that makes you different.
It's what you think about yourself
and what your God has said about you,
that really matters.

*B*efore your attitude is corrected, you can't be corrected.

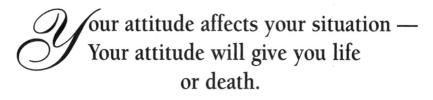

*Y*our attitude affects your situation —
Your attitude will give you life
or death.

*G*od will reach into the mess and pull
you out when you're in trouble.
Just allow Him to keep you strong
enough not to let people drag you back
into it once He gets you out.

*L*ove is eternal. It is not limited by
time. When you commit yourself to
loving someone, you make that
commitment to *all* the person is.

We are not valuable because we love
God. We are valuable because
He loves us.

*W*oman, you need to recognize what God has put *in* you. When God made you, He didn't just decorate the outside. He put some things into your feminine spirit that a man needs more than anything God put on your outside.

*T*he inner beauty that makes you valuable to God will also make you valuable to others. Some may just take longer to notice it.

*P*erhaps you feel scarred by the past.
Maybe you think you are unattractive
and unworthy. Nothing could be more untrue.
God painted a wonderful piece of artwork
one day. And that painting is you.

*G*od always has more for you
today than what you went
through yesterday.

The sinful things you may be fighting to maintain are not worth the price they cost to maintain.

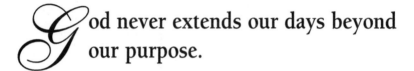

*G*od never extends our days beyond our purpose.

Those who allow their identity to be lost in circumstances will have to change with them.

*N*o matter what age you are, you have never seen it all. There are no graduations from the school of life other than death.

*B*e careful about setting your own watch. God's time is not your time. He may not come when you want Him to. But He is always right on time.

*Y*our past is paid for, even though the wounds of it have left their scars. The scars are only there to remind you that you are human. Everyone has scars.

*H*idden inside of you is a great woman who can do great exploits in His name. He wants that woman to be set free. Dare to believe that He will do what He said He would do. Unleash your faith.

*M*ost men get their feelings hurt
when they feel they have changed,
because the change is not accepted
by the woman in their life.

*M*en and women are very different. We were brought forth at different stages. The woman was the crescendo of the creation. God out-did Himself when He brought her forth.

There is nothing wrong with being
emotional. There is nothing wrong
with being able to feel. Just don't
let your emotions lead you.

*G*od wants you to pray about things you can feel. Because if it doesn't move you, chances are it won't move Him.

*G*od gave you feelings to light His altar of incense. When you burn about something in prayer by putting your feelings into it, it's like lighting the incense in the tabernacle. It goes up toward God as a sweet-smelling savor. No two prayers smell the same.

*W*hen somebody says, "I messed up, I had a baby out of wedlock, I've been divorced three times," God's not going to be touched by their holiness, He's going to be touched by the *feelings* of their infirmities.

*T*he biggest obstacle to *really* ministering to hurting people in the church is that we look on the outside of people. Don't let the clothes fool you.

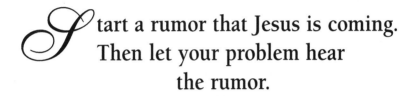

Start a rumor that Jesus is coming.
Then let your problem hear
the rumor.

*T*he real issue is, can a woman with a past touch a God in the present Who is able to change the future? It can be done!

*T*he very pain that's been tormenting and traumatizing you could be the very pain that pushes you to touch God.

As Jesus was on his way, the crowds almost crushed him. And a woman was there who had been subject to bleeding for twelve years, but no one could heal her. She came up behind him and touched the edge of his cloak, and immediately her bleeding stopped.   Luke 8:42-44 NIV

Whatever it is that you need from God, it can be done! In spite of your circumstances, it can be done.

*L*ike the woman with the issue of blood, when justice says you can't get to Him...mercy says, "Let her by."

*B*ring your bondage, secrets, night-mares, and childhood trauma to the altar and let the blood of Jesus touch them. He is able to deliver you.

*D*on't give your life to Jesus and then go back to where you came from. He wants to set you free and *keep* you free.

*S*ecrets are killing the Church because there has been no platform created for us to *just be real*. There is too much fear of being stoned.

*W*holeness doesn't come from having another person, wholeness comes from being tied in with God. Wholeness comes when He does for you what no one else could do. You are complete in Him.

*L*et the child in you cleave to the Father in Him. Be a child in the presence of God.

*S*in is not the real issue...sin is
merely how you medicate
the problem.

*N*ever allow another person's actions to control how you see yourself.

*D*on't let life kill you...Live! If you can't run, walk. If you can't walk, crawl. *But Live!*

*E*ven the worst sinner is inwardly drawn
to God, even if he doesn't serve Him.

There is something about going through dilemmas and crises' that lets us discover things about God which we would not have known under any other circumstances.

*M*any of us have tried to use God for personal gain. We have viewed God as a spiritual Santa Claus and have talked to Him only when we need something from Him. This is why many of us are constantly in problems.

*T*here are times when we are so
obsessed with our destination,
that we forget we must go through
various phases to get there.

*I*f you want to get to victory, you must be willing to go through the wilderness. This is where the people who really want to do something for God are weeded out from those who have a momentary, superficial, mundane relationship with Him.

*A*re you aware that the more the enemy fights you, the greater the indication that blessings are on the way? The enemy fights those who know who they are, and Whose they are.

*G*od is a God of plans. He is a God of order. As the God Who knows all things, He is never surprised by the attack of the enemy. He has already made a way of escape for you.

*W*hen the Scripture talks about a
peace that passes all understanding,
it is referring to a peace that is anointed.
When people look at your situation, and
then look at you, will they be confused?

*G*od loves music. When Saul was possessed with demons, David would play on his harp until the demons leaped out of Saul. There is something about the anointed music of the Holy Spirit....That is why you must be very careful about the type of music that you allow to enter your soul.

*D*on't allow anyone to take your song from your lips. Paul demonstrated that if you have a song, you can sing your way out of the jail.

*W*hatever we worship is what we ultimately end up serving.

*W*hen put into a place of prominence,
many of God's children forget
Who brought them there.

To fall is bad enough. But to fall and not cry out for help, refusing to repent for your sin, is worse than the fall itself.

*W*e sometimes find ourselves in need of not only divine, but human assistance. In fact, God usually sends other people to help us in our time of need.

*G*od is not deaf—nor is He hard of hearing. He can hear your thoughts afar off. He can hear a snail sliding through the grass in the middle of a rain storm. He knows what you are trying to say even before you say it.

*S*atan may bring false accusations against you during the trial of your faith. His perjuring principalities may bring condemning indictments. But you can't lose with the lawyer I use. Jesus has never lost a case.

God is looking for people who have enough compassion to stop and ask, "How are you today?" and then stay long enough to hear the answer.

*Q*uit acting as if you've made it on your own. God's grace and mercy have brought you through.

Whatever God declares or decrees,
He has the power to perform.

We cannot do anything without God. Don't let Satan deceive you into believing that you can make it on your own. As soon as you fall, Satan is right there whispering, "You will never get up."

Asking "why?" is not necessarily a rebellious attempt to question God's authority. "Why" is simply wanting to understand and be at one with God's reasoning.

*J*ust because the vision tarries doesn't mean God has changed His mind or given up on you. The timing of the situation may not be right for God to get the ultimate glory and benefit out of your trusting in Him.

The problem with most Christians is that we are far too impatient. If God doesn't speak in the first five minutes of our prayer time, we get up, shake ourselves off, and concede that God is not talking today.

*I*f God has spoken to you about your life and has shown you a glorious end, wait on it. If, in your waiting, you exercise faith, prayer, and patience — the vision shall surely come to pass.

*P*atience, contrary to popular belief, is not the same as waiting. Waiting is a passive posture. Patience is an active principle. It is based on the scriptural principle of persistence and perseverance.

*W*e ask for strength and God sends us difficult situations. We ask for a favor, and God gives us responsibility.

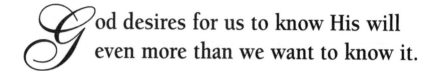

*G*od desires for us to know His will
even more than we want to know it.

*K*nowing God's divine purpose for your life is one of the greatest assets you can possess.

When you know your purpose, you won't sit and passively allow things to occur in your life that are contrary to God's purpose and vision.

*W*hen you are assured of your
purpose, you are not fearful
of men or of external personal
conflicts that attempt to hinder you.

*G*od says, "I'll do it backwards for you.
I declare the end from the beginning.
I make the beginning work into the end.
I establish purpose — then I build procedure."

*G*od's response to you is simple. Anything that is made well is made slow. "The quality must go in before His name goes on it."

*T*hings that seem impossible in the natural come to pass when we walk by faith believing in God's prophetic Word.

*T*he calling of our lives has already been determined in heaven. Your purpose in the sight of God is already an accomplished thing awaiting its fulfillment.

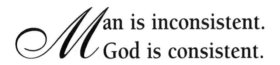

*M*an is inconsistent.
God is consistent.

*Y*ou may ask God why He allows us to go through trials and temptations. If you're not tempted by evil, how do you know you can resist evil?

*T*emptation, in and of itself, is not sin.
It is *surrendering* to temptation
that is sin.

If Jesus had not specifically called Lazarus by name, everyone and everything everywhere would have risen.

*Y*ou need to pursue your destiny
by the will and grace of God.
But understand and know assuredly
that your destiny has a price. It costs
you everything.

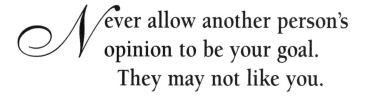

*N*ever allow another person's
opinion to be your goal.
They may not like you.

*W*hen God gets ready to bless you, He doesn't ask anybody if He can do it. He just blesses you anyway.

*D*on't go to a church that won't let you praise God.

*W*hen God makes an *appointment with you*, something awesome is going to happen.

No power can hold you, no demon can stop you....Give God what He wants and He will make every enemy leave you alone.

*F*ear traps time and holds it hostage
in a prison of icy anxiety.

*I*t is He alone Whom we must trust to see the very worst in us, yet still think the very best of us. It is simply the love of a Father.

I believe the Church has confused *conviction with condemnation....* *Conviction* leads us to a place of deliverance and change. *Condemnation* leads us to the gallows of despair and hopelessness.

*W*e are properly draped and dressed to come into the presence of a holy God only because His accepted Son, Jesus Christ, has wrapped us in His own identity.

I began to realize the great truth that the blood of Christ doesn't just reach backwards into the bleakness of my past debauchery — it also has the power to cover my ongoing struggles!

*W*hen Mary, the sinner, came and washed Jesus' feet with her tears, some mocked Jesus and discredited Him.... It wasn't that Jesus didn't know the hands that washed His feet had done wrong.... It was that He didn't care!

*W*e need to lay ourselves before Him
and seek His face in the beauty of
holiness — the holiness that
produces wholeness.

The greatest place to preach isn't in our great meetings with swelling crowds and lofty recognitions. The greatest place to preach is in the trenches, in the foxholes and the hogpens of life.

*O*h, thou man or woman of great passion, driven by intense feelings and desires, you often wrestle with your ambitious nature. Hear me and hear me well: You don't want to kill your passion — you just need to redirect it toward a godly vision.

*I*f we exist without passion, we slump
into a state of stagnation that hinders
us from achieving the purpose
of God in our lives.

*I*t is the burning effect of a vision that causes us to escape destruction.

*T*here is absolutely no substitute for the syrupy nectar of human experience. It is experience that seasons the future relationships God has in store for us.

To never trust again is to live on the pinnacle of a tower. You may feel safe from life's threatening grasp, but you will be so detached from life that you may soon lose consciousness of people, places, dates, and events.

*I*f the angels were to stroll through the earth with the Creator and ask, "Which house is yours?" He would pass by all the mansions, cathedrals, temples and castles. Then unashamedly, He would point at you and me and say, "That house is Mine!"

The very best of us camouflage the very worst in us with religious colloquialisms that reduce Christianity to more of an act than an attitude.

The renewal of the old man is a daily exercise of the heart. It progressively strengthens the character day by day, not overnight!

It is when we strip away the facade of the superficial and ask God to bring about the supernatural that we experience the real power of God.

*W*e must learn how to be as open
about our failures as we are about
our successes. Without this kind of honesty,
we create a false image that causes
others to needlessly struggle.

*W*hen you find someone who can see your flaws and your under-developed character, *and love you in spite of it all*, you are blessed.

*R*epentance comes because of the unfailing love of a perfect God, a God Who cares for the cracked vases that others would have discarded.

*I*t is to the distraught heart that seeks so desperately for a place of refuge that we extend soft hands and tender words.

This "dippity-doo, a little dab will do you" mentality that we preach is not scriptural at all. We need God's treatment every day. We are not a finished product.

*J*esus' love was *so awesome* that it could only be depicted by the morbidity of His dying.

*O*ur ministers are dying of loneliness
because they feel obligated to
maintain some false image of perfection
in order to be of service in our society.

*C*an you imagine what the disciples thought when Jesus ended supper and laid aside His garments? How could a person of His stature stoop so low? I tell you, He never stood as tall as He did when He stooped so low to bless those men whom He had taught.

*E*very person who finds real purpose will sooner or later go through some series of adversities that will cause them to let go of the temporal and cleave to the eternal.

*T*rue worship is born when true
sacrifice occurs. When we lay
upon the altar some bleeding object
that we thought we would keep for
ourselves, that's worship.

*Y*our ministry truly becomes effective
when you know that there is precious
little difference between the people
you serve and yourself.

With joy we draw water from the wells of salvation! But what good is that water if we fail to use it to wash away the weariness of someone's journey?

About the Author

T.D. Jakes is the senior pastor and founder of The Potter's House Church in Dallas, Texas. Transcending all social and gender barriers, his message of healing and restoration is broadcast nationally into millions of homes. Bishop Jakes ministers frequently in massive crusades and conferences across this nation. He is also a highly celebrated author with several bestselling books to his credit.

To contact T.D. Jakes write:

Jakes Ministries
P.O. Box 210887
Dallas, Texas 75211

Additional copies of this book and other book titles
from **ALBURY PUBLISHING** are
available at your local bookstore.

Albury Publishing
P.O. Box 470406
Tulsa, Oklahoma 74147-0406

In Canada books are available from:

Word Alive
P. O. Box 670
Niverville, Manitoba
CANADA ROA 1EO